Your life:

Live it

Love it!

© Johanna Mattsson 2014

ISBN - 978-91-637-7244-3

Storuman Tryckeri & Reklam AB

The author

Johanna Mattsson travelled from the north of Sweden to France after graduating from high school to attend a private business school in Nice. She has a Master in International Marketing Strategies and also studied the MBA program at Waseda University in Tokyo. She has always combined studying with projects and it was the French luxury company Louis Vuitton & Moët Hennessy that influenced her to leave Europe for Tokyo. She worked within the private banking sector throughout Asia before moving back to Europe. Besides her various business projects she teaches sales and international marketing at a private business school in Stockholm.

Contents:

Introduction

ROAD TO "DAMASCUS"

I felt a tear running down my cheek though I was fighting hard not to show anything. A conflict was raging in my head and I couldn't stop tears from coming.

Paul, my boss, just looked at me with his big teddy bear eyes. The Chairman and founder of the financial service company I was working for in Singapore had always been able to see right through me, ever since we first met in Tokyo two years ago. Here I was, a successful financial adviser to the expat market with one of the largest financial advisory firms in Asia, providing comprehensive wealth management solutions to investors, regularly travelling the region to manage my Scandinavian and French clients' portfolios.
And I had suddenly realised that all the goals I'd been chasing since the age of eight and across the globe were not what I really wanted. I had spent the last year travelling to every Asian country, beach and fashionable resort I fancied, convincing myself that this was the life to lead.

I still felt so empty.

Paul was a great man and a good manager and I'd had an inclination that our meeting this afternoon would have an effect on me. I knew I was good at what I did and I knew he thought I was great, but I was still scared because, deep down, my tough shell was all a charade. I didn't know who I was anymore or how I wanted to spend my life. Everything had gone so fast and I'd experienced so much that I was at a loss at what to put down on my list of things to do or places to visit.

I had actually been too focused and now I didn't know where I belonged any more. Paul would force me to face my weaknesses. I knew he was going to ask me to find my own path, to find what I really felt passionate about.

Earlier that same morning I had met Andrew, one of my senior colleagues, at the coffee shop opposite my office building. He was crying. Andrew, my mentor, my rock at work, never cried nor showed any emotion. It turned out he had just lost about everything in a divorce settlement. He had earned loads of money but it all had gone on nice cars, trips, boats and an expensive house. He had no liquid assets once the divorce was finalised, and that was why he was crying.

How tragic! He was crying over the loss of material things, not the breakdown of his marriage! Listening to him made me realise!

I had just spent the last year spending ridiculous sums of money on travel which had actually meant nothing more to me than an opportunity to visit great places. Was this really my true purpose in life and what I truly felt passionate about? Was my life all about the next deal which could be measured in a new watch?

This had to change. I could just feel the panic growing up my spine.

Chapter 1

THE ROAD OF LIFE OFTEN
STARTS WITH A QUESTION

"There is a difference between interest and commitment. When you are interested in doing something, you do it only when it is convenient. When you are committed to something, you accept no excuses; only results."
- Kenneth Blanchard

I managed to walk away from my meeting with Paul without starting to cry, although he'd probably seen a tear or two roll down my cheek. I just couldn't hold them back. I had to find some sort of inner peace. I wasn't sad because my life was going badly, on the contrary in fact, and I had a great career too. I just didn't recognise myself in the role that I was currently playing, nor could I feel any passion for what I was doing. I went back to my apartment, packed a duffel bag and walked down to the dock where boats departed for Malaysia's Tioman Islands. I needed some peace and quiet and what could be better than a tranquil island with nothing but my own thoughts for company.
Although I had demonstrated great commitment to my career and had achieved my business goals on an international scale, I realised that I was becoming increasingly bored and was finding it more and more difficult to justify why I should be working any harder.

Sometimes we think we want something because of the influence of people who surround us, or the kind of life we're living. Sooner or later reality catches up with us and we start to think for ourselves.

Our journeys often start with the question "why?".

It may sound like the simplest question in the world but it's not: if it was, everyone would ask "why?" before they started chasing their goals.
If the reason why is sincere, then you will move forward no matter what you encounter on the way.

Here are a few examples from "the real world".

Virgin Group founder Richard Branson once found himself stranded on Beef Island, in the British Virgin Islands, when trying to catch a flight to Puerto Rico. Instead of just accepting the situation he started talking to fellow passengers, who were also seeking the best way of leaving the island. He made some calls and ended up chartering a plane. He then divided the cost by the number of seats and sold tickets to the others stuck alongside him. In doing so, he discovered that the actual cost of flying was far less than what the public was normally charged. This resulted in the founding of Virgin Airways.

IKEA creator Ingvar Kamprad, once asked himself why designer furnishings were so expensive and limited to a very small market. He started investigating how he could offer a wide range of well designed and functional items at prices affordable to the lowest income earners. When an employee later suggested that removing table legs would make them flat and thus fit more easily into a car, IKEA's revolutionary flat pack concept was born.

Both cases demonstrate what can happen when someone with an entrepreneurial spirit poses the question "why"? I once interviewed one of the many successful entrepreneurs in the Japanese automobile industry who told me that once you've asked your first why and achieved your first goals, you just keep going.
Of course success doesn't just happen because you have a goal and you know why you have it. You have to put the effort in to make it work!

I was on my way to a small island off the east coast of Malaysia. I had goals in my life, I just didn't know why they were so important to me. This is what had thrown me off course and prevented me from taking real action.

I do know though why I put this book together. I wanted to share my story with you. I want you to understand that only you can chose what you want to accomplish. I have been told so many times that I can't do this or that, but if there is one thing I want to emphasise, it is that you will go that extra mile if you have passion and a belief in yourself. The greater your passion, the quicker you will start to achieve your goals.

I met Cathy for the first time in Nice, France, while conducting interviews for my Bachelor thesis on successful businesswomen. She was the daughter of a very successful Scandinavian businessman who had known my father and normally never gave interviews. However she made an exception for me because of my thesis. Cathy had been sent to the famous Ecole Hôtelière de Lausanne with a view to going into the family business, just as her brothers had done. The problem was that she was tired of having everything arranged for her by others and wanted to achieve success on her own merit. After graduating from school she started working within the Swiss hotel industry. Within a few years she had worked her way up from the post of receptionist to hotel management.

Not wanting to use her family name and ties, she adopted her mother's maiden name when applying for further jobs. After several years she left Switzerland for the Mediterranean where she built up her own portfolio comprising several hotel and tourist businesses. Cathy adored her family but, just like her parents had done before her, she needed to create something of her own. I thought she was amazing because not only did she manage to establish a number of corporations, she did so without using her family status. That is what true passion is all about.

Even though these examples are all business-related, they could also be applied at a personal level, such as finding your true love, losing weight or becoming healthier - just about anything.

All whys are not easy to distinguish or to act upon. In my health goals (see chapter 2), I stated that I wanted to climb Mt Blanc before May. It turned out that the achievement of reaching the summit was not as important to me as the training required beforehand. The experience also taught me how to balance health with a busy work schedule, something I believe in very strongly.

Don't be afraid of making the wrong decisions: as long as you keep going forward you are moving closer towards your goals.

Chapter 2

GOALS!

"If you don't know where you are going, you might wind up someplace else." - Yogi Berra

The journey that brought me to my life-changing moment in Singapore began at an early age. I still remember the day in second grade when it started.

Our teacher Mrs Holm asked us to draw a picture and write about what we wanted to be when we grew up. When I presented my drawing, everybody laughed at me. All the other children had done really beautiful paintings of ponies, Barbie dolls, police officers, doctors and so on. I, on the other hand, had drawn a woman with a briefcase, dollar signs around her head and a globe. No one seemed to understand my drawing. That was probably not surprising as I wasn't any good at art but I thought the dollar signs and the globe got the point across. I told my teacher and classmates that when I grew up I wanted to be an international businesswoman making loads of money and travelling the world.

No one understood. How could an eight year-old be interested in exchange rates and money?

Children truly believe they can be anything. They dream about becoming doctors, lawyers or football professionals, no matter what kind of society or from which social class they come, and parents encourage them to do so. It has been calculated that we receive 60% of our lifetime's encouragements before reaching the age of three. For a baby, the feat of just standing up brings cheers of appreciation and encouragement, but after a few years those cheers turn into corrections and the older we get, the number of people cheering us on becomes fewer and fewer. It is quite scary to realise that the closer you get to achieving your goals, the less encouragement and support you will receive along the way.

But why does this happen?

As we grow up we allow ourselves to be influenced by people and society around us, leading to doubts being raised in our minds. However, I strongly believe that these doubts are no more than figments of our imagination. If we do not let people interrupt our dreams and distract us from our internal focus, each and every one of us can achieve the lifestyle we aspire to. As adults, we might have to work a little harder to keep those dreams alive, but they are just as achievable as they were when we were children.

When I realised that I had lost my passion for earning millions of dollars, I started talking to as many of the world's successful businesspeople as possible to see if I could reignite it in some way.

The first thing I learned from them was how vital it was to clarify my goals which should, I discovered, be very precise and encompass a time span ranging from one month to 10 years.

It is also necessary to include at least two goals that will generate immediate results. This will prevent you from putting things off until "tomorrow".
And the act of writing them down makes them real and vital.

When I got back home from school after our class presentations on that cold winter day, I told my father how everybody had laughed at me. He responded by asking me to recreate the drawing I had done in school and then to hang it up on my bedroom wall. He pointed out that the only way to put the others in their place was achieve to my dreams. I walked quietly up to my room and did just as he had told me with the picture. I let it hang there until I moved out ten years later.

There is a tangible difference between just thinking about your goals and actually writing them down. I don't profess to know why this is so, but what I do know is that it works. I have always written down my goals, as have all the interesting and successful people I have met over the years.

In his book, *What they don't teach you in Harvard Business School*, Mark McCormack describes a 1979 study conducted on graduate students at a Harvard MBA program. They were asked if they had set clear, written goals for their futures and made plans to accomplish them. The results showed that only 3% of the graduates had written goals and plans; 13% had goals but hadn't put them down on paper, while 84% had no specific goals at all.

Ten years later, the same group was interviewed again and the 13% with unwritten goals were earning, on average, twice as much as the 84% who had no goals at all. However the 3% who had clear, written goals were earning, on average, ten times as much as the rest of the group put together.

Virtually all businesses have written business plans and strategies as these are essential for continued development. People, too, need the same in order to achieve their goals. It's entirely possible that if you don't create your own you will find and try to use someone else's, but this kind of copying will probably have the same outcome as a company that copies its competitors. You won't last long!
Whether it involves copying a business or a person, such an approach seldom leads to any lasting success. Doing something without a true purpose means passion is lacking. That's more than likely to result in boredom, which leads to inaction and then, invariably, failure.

Here is an example that demonstrates the benefits of writing down your goals.

I once attended a business school where our professor in business strategies asked us to write down our personal mission statements. A few years later, when I was launching my first business I went through my old school books and found the following:

Personal Mission Statement

"By always setting higher goals and exploring new adventures, I will one day be the CEO of an international company, breaking new ground while being able to communicate in seven different languages. Living close to nature will keep me focused. My ambition and willingness to fight will always make me choose the harder way of doing things. By doing so I will continuously improve myself and, in the long term, overcome my competitors."

Johanna Mattsson, February 10, 2002

Five years later I could speak six languages, had lived in four countries and become the CEO of an international company. I was also living at a ski resort. Nothing had been accomplished without hard work, nor had it always been easy. But I had carried my written goals in my purse and decided not to give up until I had tried absolutely everything I possibly could to achieve what was on that piece of paper before I turned 30. You haven't failed until you give up!

If you haven't written down your goals yet, now is the time! Put on some good music and let your pen do the rest. I know it sounds simple - why not just give it a try?
Remember to write down what you'd like to accomplish in every section of your life. Being successful in business at the cost of your health, family or the one you love is not proper success. A truly successful and wealthy person finds balance in life by achieving their goals without sacrificing themselves.

It is important that your goals are measurable and given a time limit. Continuously postponing until "tomorrow" won't get you far. Write down as much as you can without thinking too much about it. Go on - just do it!
There is no right or wrong in what you write, as long as what you have written is true to you.

Look at the following examples of what my goals looked like a few years ago.

---

1. Business

    * Only work with things I think are fun and lift me higher

    * Only work with people, clients and tasks I feel passionate about

    * Only work with things that give me the freedom to grow and experience life while helping others

    * Expand my business by 10% each quarter starting May 5, without increasing numbers of hours at work

---

2. Finance

    * Increase the gap between money coming in and money being spent by at least 20% annually

    * Increase average "Fun & Play" account by 10% within the next quarter by generating a higher turnover from my investments

    * Increase average investment turnover from 10-15% within next year

---

3. Family

* Take my family and friends on four trips and new adventures during the year

* Buy a house by the ocean within the next three years from today

* Buy a new ski chalet within the next five years from today

* Buy a new apartment abroad within the next three years

4. Health

* Spend at least 10 hours week training

* Climb Mt Blanc in May

* Climb Mt Fuji within the next year and spend time in Japan

* Visit the Base Camp of Mt Everest within the next five years

5. Travel

* Visit Paris again within the next year

* Rent a house for two weeks next summer in Provence

* Book a skiing trip to Whistler within the coming year

* Try something new in the Caribbean within the next two years

Now it's your turn. Take a moment and start to write down what you want your life to include in the next few days, weeks, months or years. Remember to ensure you include a few things that you want to see happening within the short-term. Then you won't have the excuse of being able to postpone everything until a later date!

You can use the topics suggested here or choose your own. A copy of the goal sheet is found the appendix section of the book.

Chapter 3

ENJOYING THE MOMENT

"Man alone has the power to transform his thought into physical reality; man alone can dream and make his dreams come true." - Napoleon Hill

I had loved every moment of my experience in Asia. It had been a magical journey ever since my arrival at Tokyo Narita Airport. I had grown so much in such a short space of time that I sometimes found it hard keeping up with myself. Focused on my goals of becoming someone my parents could be proud of and not screaming all the time to gain the attention of my father, had resulted in me becoming totally lost. I just wanted to be the same kind of successful businessperson he had always been to me. Now I was sitting under the sun at an amazing bar in Singapore with cash in my pockets, fancy suits, and the global lifestyle I always wanted but emptiness in my heart. Was this it? How could I improve on this? How could I grow? Was this really the life I wanted?

My journey had started some twenty years earlier at school when I was eight. I had presented my drawing depicting my future which had prompted howls of laughter from my classmates. Actually, laughter could be heard every time I was forced to read aloud. My body temperature would rocket as if I was in a sauna and my heart would beat faster and heavier. My childhood poor reading and writing abilities resulted in me listening to the teachers and memorising every thing they said. I would ask my parents to rent historical movies about the great wars and memorise the dates. When there was an English programme on TV I would stick tape across the bottom of the screen to avoid reading the subtitles. My family would even travel to the destinations we were studying at school in order to get a real feel for their histories.

It was not until, aged sixteen, I completely failed a national Swedish language test that my family began to understand when I said the letters moved when I looked at them. I had tried to explain before at school and asked to be tested for dyslexia, but the teachers' answer was always the same: I was too smart to have any problems with reading or writing. They thought my high energy levels and lack of focus were why I skipped words. If only I could focus more, my grades would improve, they maintained.

I could have just accepted this verdict and become a victim of the educational system, but I didn't. I chose to find my own solutions and ways around the problem. I would highlight my books in different colours and memorise TV documentaries. As a teenager I had to choose between staying home alone studying or hanging out with friends.

Instead of being made to feel sorry for myself by those laughing at me, I felt sorry for the teachers who thought that only stupid people could be dyslexic. I reasoned that they were never going to go any further in life than the local school where they worked or the neighbourhood in which they had lived for the last ten years, and I just kept dreaming about my tomorrow.

I still memorise all my speeches just so I won't have to look down at my notes. The up side of this, however, is that once I have learnt a speech or a lecture, I do not have to refer to it again.

While at university I met dyslexics who would use their condition as an excuse for bad grades or written results. I see this as a way of avoiding the disappointment of personal failure. It's true that books take more time to read and that I need to be much more focused and preferably undisturbed, but nothing is impossible. There are no excuses that are as good as the ones we make for ourselves.

We all have the option of accepting our particular handicaps or fighting for what we believe in.

At an early age I learned how to "sell" my ideas and opinions to teachers who were teaching the subjects I was interested in. I moved from being a laughed at outsider to an insider. I became someone who knew what the teachers wanted. I became someone who made up my own rules and walked my own way. I cannot really remember how it happened, but I actually became the financial adviser for a few of my teachers at university who would later introduce me to important business networks and future investment opportunities.

My fellow university and business school students were focused on getting the highest grades and the best trainee places with a view to becoming the most successful employees. I, however, focused on creating a strong network, collecting what I thought I needed to know in order to become a free agent. I knew that I was going to have the world as my playground.

If you have ever been to a business networking event, the speaker will often ask you to meet as many people as possible. There might even be a prize for the one who collects the most business cards.
How many business cards have you received that just ended up in the trash?

I strongly believe that successful networking is not about the number of people you connect with, but about what those you have met can do for you. I didn't network with all the teachers as there was no point being part of a group that didn't interest me. But my genuine interest in what some teachers did and the lifestyles they had, did lead to invitations to stay at their homes on the Côte D'Azur.

The American mathematician, John Allen Paulo, says that uncertainty is the only certainty there is, and knowing how to live with insecurity is the only security. I think he's right because most of us are afraid of not knowing what tomorrow will bring. Take what happened to the employees of two large and highly respected companies, who probably thought they had jobs for life.

On December 19th, 2011, the 3,950 employees of Swedish car manufacturer SAAB were told the company had declared bankruptcy. The workforce, accounting for 20% of the local population, had lost its single source of income overnight.

ENRON, which used to be one of the world's largest electrical companies employing over 22,000 people, went bankrupt in December 2001. Due to "creative accounting" it had lost everything. There were neither salaries nor pension funds available to employees who were sent home the day the bankruptcy was announced.

Despite the fact that these sort of collapses still occur, most people rarely think about the risk of being an employee as opposed to being an employer.

Don't be fooled into the false security of a steady job. The truth is that there are risks in everything we do, it is just that the degree of risk can be debated and our perceptions of what is risky vary from person to person. Some of us are satisfied with just waking up each morning knowing that our five-day working week will generate a steady income. Others love throwing themselves at every new opportunity that comes along without knowing where it might take them. It is important to know what drives you and why. Frankly, it's not as easy as I make it sound and I understand if people are really confused about life, but isn't that just because most of us never sit down and draw our own personalised map of where we are going?

If you wrote down financial freedom as one of your goals I believe you are more likely to achieve it by creating your own business. If you don't, you will be hired by someone else to create their wealth; your financial goals will probably not be part of that person's dream!

The bottom line is that people are employed to help a business owner fulfil his or her dream. Most business advice books say you should get 80% of your turnover from 20% of your work. No matter if this is true or not, the first rule is to spend less then you earn, which in today's society is easer said than done. You'd think that many more of us would be aware of this simple fact, but levels of credit have never been as high as they are today.

Véronique, whom I first met as a lecturer in finance at the business school I attended, taught me at an early stage that wealth accumulation is all about taking calculated financial risks, working hard, being disciplined and keeping focused on your dreams. She also taught me that there is a clear and very significant correlation between willingness to take financial risk and net worth. When calculating financial risks for any investments you always have to take the cost of inaction into account. I have always carried this thought with me because even if some risks seem dangerous, the alternative might be zero income.

Remember, no matter whether you opt to be an employee or employer, your productivity and creativity will be greater if you love what you are doing. In fact, there is a direct positive correlation between the love of one's vocation and level of net worth.

You do not really have to be that smart to understand that just by focusing on what you really love doing you will become more successful.

However, for most people this seems difficult, otherwise we would not have so many earning just enough to survive. I am not saying that everyone who struggles to live comfortably is choosing to be in that position, I am just trying to point out that by establishing your goals and the reasons why you should reach them, you will be compelled to act. This applies to anyone, no matter how rich or poor.

Only the fear of failure can stop you from moving forward. Fear comes in all forms and we usually camouflage it as something else. "I don't have time," or "I'll do it tomorrow," are just two common excuses. If you are nervous about going ahead because you are unsure of the outcome, write down the worst possible consequences if you do.

Would your life really end?

Think first about the worst possible scenario and then about the goals, aspirations and possibilities you will lose as a result of this fear.

The truth is that what we usually fear the most is, actually, what we need to do the most.
I believe that one of the many obstacles that we have to overcome is the fear of holding uncomfortable conversations. Even if you don't always succeed, facing a tricky situation will generate more confidence. Respect each and every challenge but don't be afraid. It's just another opportunity to grow.

Herbert Bayard Swope, a journalist and Pulitzer prizewinner once said: *"I can't give you a super fine formula for success, but I can give you a formula for failure: try to please everybody all the time."*

I once undertook research into why there were more female managers in Italy and France compared to Sweden, a country known for gender equality. As part of this study I met some interesting women who had built up successful businesses and careers remarkably quickly.

Veronique, whom I mentioned earlier, had been the youngest ever manager of a hedge fund department of a Luxembourg bank. When I asked her how she stayed ahead of the game, she said: "Some people just seem to forget that the world market does not go to sleep at 5pm nor does it take six weeks vacation every year. "

She didn't mean that you have to work around the clock or skip holidays in order to be successful, she meant that you have understand how the world functions. Because of the time differences in America, Asia and Europe, she would arrive at her desk early to get updates on how Asia was trading, or stay late to see how a big decision in Europe affected the American market. Instead of taking six weeks off in one go, she would take weeks or weekends off throughout the year. In this way she was able to take her allotted time off but still stay ahead of the game.

Cathy's family had run an international hotel business for generations. She said that the difference between those who made it and those who didn't could be likened to someone driving a car towards traffic lights.

"When the lights are amber, there are those who start breaking even before they reach the crossroads just to get a signal on how to act," she said. "Then there are those who accelerate in order to get over the line just before the lights turn red."

Cathy meant that many Swedish women slow down and start to look for signs and opinions when important decisions are to be made. They don't like stepping on too many toes. In comparison, French women accelerate right through, taking the risk. This is not only about women being different to men or differences between individual women, but also about cultural differences in management and decision-making. Cathy, however, believed that no matter where you are, you'll never get very far without taking risks or if you worry about upsetting others.

My research showed that female managers in France and Italy worried less about what others thought than those in Sweden did. Before making a decision, Swedish managers, I discovered, would consult their employees or colleagues far more than their French or Italian counterparts who would just act and take the consequences later.
Even in societies where to stand out from the crowd is deemed socially unacceptable, you're not going to get very far if you don't follow your instincts and do what is best for YOU in each

and every situation. And what is best today may not be so good tomorrow, but that is one of the risks we have to take.

Think of this the next time you are about to do a sales pitch or try a new business idea. If you don't go through with it, someone else will. Conditions are never perfect and "later" is a disease that will ensure that your dreams go to the grave with you. If it's important to you, just do it and adjust your methods along the way.

Stay focused on your goals.

Your reasons "why" that you wrote down in the first section of this book should help you stay focused at all times. Business markets are moving faster than ever and to stay ahead of the game and take advantage of any new opportunities that arise, you need to remind yourself of those goals.

How you treat your body, mind and business are of equal importance. Forgetting to plan what to put in your fridge will usually result in fast food purchases on the way home. Just take five or ten minutes to check what's in your fridge and plan the week's meals. You will buy healthier and cheaper. I know I make it sound so simple but that's because it is.

Most of us are good at a handful of things but not so good at a lot of others. Have fun concentrating on what your strengths are instead of trying to shore up all your weaknesses.

Why would you want to stay ahead of the game? The answer is pretty simple. Catching up is always so much harder. Imagine the man who starts a race 20 metres behind Usain Bolt. Not only will he have to catch up with the fastest man on earth, he'll have to pass him.

During her first year at work Veronique only put in a few extra hours per day, but they gave her the focus she needed to stay on top. She has since been able to maintain this distance with her colleagues who are now having to work extra hours just to catch her up. While they are learning from her, she is focussing on improving her results and leading the way.

In Japan there is a saying that if a nail stands out higher than the others, hammer it down until it's even with the rest. The truth is that the world is full of people who are afraid to stand out from the crowd and that means it is relatively easy for you. There is less competition for larger goals as fewer people dare to chase them. That's why you have to aim for higher goals, no matter in which society or culture you live.

So aim for big things, push the boat out and enjoy the challenge - that is the key!

Chapter 4

FEAR OF REJECTION

"Your biography is not your destiny, your decisions are." - Oprah Winfrey

Anna's soft lips touched mine. I shook uncontrollably as we kissed for the very first time, and then again and again.
The following morning I awoke to feel fear crawling up my spine. What had I done?
Anna was my best friend. We did everything together, our boyfriends were also best friends and we had known each other for ages.
I told myself it was probably just one of those drunken experiences and part of growing up.

We would never speak about that night again, but Anna had made me feel complete in a way I never had before. The question was, how could something I'd been brought up to believe was so bad make me feel so amazing and alive? And how could I ever find the courage to tell my parents?

I was supposed to be a great student and an even better athlete. I was supposed to fall in love with a great prince, not a princess! I imagined my mother's condemnation echoing through my head: "This is a shameful disgrace, we don't have people like this in our family."

This was just a phase, so there was no point in telling my family about something that soon enough would be nothing more than a memory. If I kept on dating good-looking boys I would fall back into what I had been brought up to be believe as normality. Or so I thought.

It would take a further six years of internal conflict before I learned how to handle and accept my feelings. And it would be another three years before I had the courage to write them in an email to my parents and press send.

There will always be times when we stumble upon opportunities and chances that present us with difficult choices.
We can take the easy way out or we can focus on taking a path that changes our destiny. The sooner we realise that we are the authors of our own future, the less time we will waste trying to fit into someone else's plans and the more time we will have to enjoy the wonders of life's journey.

Every circumstance can be seen differently, depending on the individual. You can either enjoy tackling a challenge and being seen as the right person to do it or, fearing rejection and, or failure, you can take the safe option.

A good example of the same circumstance being seen differently by different people is illustrated in Walter Isaac's biography *Steve Jobs*. The Apple founder recalled the time he told the girl who lived across the street that he was adopted and how she said that was because his real parents didn't want him. When an upset Steve told his parents what she'd said, they looked straight at him and told him the exact opposite: they had carefully chosen him because he was unique and just what they wanted.[1]

All the successful people I have met have learnt to overcome their fear of rejection rather than let it dictate their lives.
They have learnt how to sell the same idea over and over again, no matter how many refusals they receive, until they finally get someone to hear or see them.
Did you know, for example, that Colonel Sanders, the founder of KFC (Kentucky Fried Chicken) is said to have been turned down more than 1,000 times before he finally found someone who said yes to selling his trademarked fried chicken?
Today KFC is an American icon, as well as the world's largest chicken restaurant franchise and the second biggest selling restaurant chain.[2]
What's more, Colonel Sanders began his journey towards fast food success at the ripe old age of 65, so don't let anyone tell you that you're too young or too old for something.

When I joined a British financial firm in Tokyo as a

---

[1] Steve Jobs by Walter Isaacson 2011, p.80 Hachette Digital

[2] *a b c* Lopez, Linette (13 July 2011). "The 10 Largest Restaurant Chains In America". *Business Insider.* Retrieved 27 February 2013.

strategic advisor, my previous financial experience was zero but the company's boss, whom I had met at a party, saw something in me that he wanted.

I quickly grasped the opportunities my new job offered; financial knowledge, the chance to meet many of Asia's business leaders and to travel the region.

It was commission-based work where, as a team, we could only progress if we provided our clients with suitable opportunities in which to invest. I quickly learnt how to do the calculations and regarded every rejection as one step closer to a yes.

I might not have been a Howard Schultz, who is said to have been turned down by 242 banks before he found one that was willing in invest in Starbucks, but I did hear "no" more than "yes".

I calculated how many times, on average, my ideas and solutions had to be turned down in order for me to finally close a deal.

My success in my new career gave me a self-confidence I had never had before. I was "flying" and enjoying life with friends. We were young and free, with cash in our pockets that enabled us spend lavishly and travel the South Pacific.

However, there's a limit to the amount of happiness money can buy and I soon reached it. As I mentioned before, many of us believe that having enough money will solve all our problems, whereas the reality is that money may just delay the solution. And that's what happened in my case.

You may be a brilliant businessperson and establish a successful company or provide corporations with fabulous solutions, but if you are not complete as a person you will always be seeking something else to achieve inner satisfaction.

After three years of globetrotting I realised I was emotionally empty.

I had told my sister I was gay long before anyone else and she had proven to be a great support, but I didn't want anyone else in the family to know. Even when I was ready, I didn't dare to call my parents or my brother. I just summoned my courage and sent them that email. The realisation that I was gay and would not live the kind of life I'd been brought up to believe was the right one, was an enormous shock. It took me a long time to accept my sexuality. My success in Asia gave me the strength to confront the issue of opening up and finally letting my whole family know how I really lived my life.

"Many of life's failures are people who did not realise how close they were to success when they gave up."
- Thomas Edison

Rejection of your business ideas or your lifestyle makes you reflect deeply about yourself and your views. What triggers your emotions? How do you feel when you analyse them? If you throw caution to the wind, what will your life look like in ten years' time?

What are you gaining by sticking to traditional beliefs that are, more than likely, holding you back?
For me, I was desperate to keep the love of my parents and I was terrified that they would turn their backs on me if they found out I was not the kind of daughter they had wanted.

The only solution is to go forward.

There's no doubt, however, that maintaining that momentum in the face of heavy criticism from all sides is a major challenge. You need to be prepared for the day when not everybody will be as happy as you, including those whom you love, and who love you best. They may think that your move is too drastic and involves too many risks.
Only you can prove them wrong but before you do, ask yourself if you will be able to spend the rest of your life in a way that will make others happy or if you have what it takes to achieve inner happiness, despite what people think?
Your inner spirit is a treasure that is infinitely greater than anything anyone else can offer you, so put your fear aside and grasp what the world has to offer!

Chapter 5

LIFT YOURSELF HIGHER!

"Surround yourself only with people who are going to lift you higher." - Oprah Winfrey

I reached into the pocket of my wife's jacket. She had asked me to get her wallet and buy some things for a cozy evening together at home. It was a cold December night and I had just returned after spending three weeks on a life-changing leadership course in California. A quiet night in after all the dining out I had done was just perfect. However, instead of the wallet, I found a beautiful card. Christmas was coming up and, being curious, I couldn't stop myself from reading. It was a beautiful love letter expressing deep emotion - but it didn't look like my wife's handwriting. It was signed: "Soon it's only you and I again."

I think I knew it immediately from the first line but I did not want to understand. The card was not meant for me, it was an expression of love from someone else to my wife. Standing there with her jacket in one hand and the card in the other, it felt like someone was sticking needles right into my heart. I felt myself falling. I wanted to sink through the floor and disappear.
Despite the thousands of questions flooding my brain, I couldn't find the words to say anything. I tried to stay as calm and focused as I could.

On my flight home from America I had been thinking about how lucky I was to share my life with someone who truly loved me. Now everything had changed dramatically. Had I done anything wrong in the last few months? Were there any signs I should have been aware of?
I was so full of pain it hurt to breathe. I couldn't speak. I walked out and ended up at a friend's house for the night.

In the days that followed I knew I would somehow have to pick myself up and carry on, but I didn't want to as I was hurting so much. A door had been slammed right in my face and I couldn't find the words to express myself.

"One day you will wake up and there won't be any more time to do the things you've always wanted. Do it now."
- Paulo Coelho

When life throws you a curveball it is so easy to talk about why you are not where you want to be, or bemoan why things are as they are, instead of getting yourself together and doing something about it.

To cut a long story short, my response to my marriage collapse was to go to the gym where I could work all the anger and negative energy out of my system and create something positive from it. I quickly became mentally (and physically) stronger and, having found a greater peace of mind through sport, discovered I was in a much happier place than I had been for quite some time.

I am not saying my transformation was without pain. Some of my friends doubted that I had ever been truly in love as it seemed as though I'd rebounded too quickly. However, I firmly believe that recovery from any setback, emotional or otherwise, is not about how long it takes but the way you get through it and that things happen for us, not to us.

A marriage break-up or job loss is a greater shock if you are caught by surprise. But being unaware that something isn't quite right is not unusual: apportioning blame is never a solution. Remembering what was good and focusing on the future is the way forward. In my case, I decided to act on the feelings I had; that's the kind of person I am. If those circumstances or my marriage were not meant to be I didn't want to spend another minute worrying about them while life passed me by.

I am always meeting people who tell me I am so lucky to have seen such a lot of the world and done so much.

I am no smarter than anyone else. If anything, I allow myself to make more mistakes than most - but I admit to making them and try to learn my lessons. While most people work hard not to make mistakes, I get right out there looking for new ones! You cannot improve your future if you are not willing to try something new. Doing things differently often carries a risk of making mistakes, but then you learn from them. What you do is infinitely more important than how you do it.

Doing something unimportant successfully does not make it important. Although it helps you practice your methods or routine, it hardly tests you to the limit. But if you never allow yourself to fall, getting back up immediately becomes much harder and will take a lot longer.

Change doesn't happen by itself, it requires the right circumstances, the right state of mind.
In the first chapter I asked you to put on a piece of favourite music while writing down your goals; listening to music that makes you happy automatically puts you in a better working frame of mind.

Even though I had been devastated by my marriage breakdown, I forced myself to get into a better state by listening to great music, training hard in the gym and feeling the power the workouts gave me. I rewrote my lifeline through the steady building of a new strategy. I could feel happy and strong once more.

If you want to achieve success, go to the source.
When asked why he robbed banks, infamous American criminal Willy Sutton replied: "I want money so I go where the money is."

I needed energy and vitality so I headed to the gym where people were bursting with both and focused. Soon I was fizzing with the same amount of energy as my personal trainer.

"You will be more disappointed by the things you did not do than by the ones you did do. So throw off the bowlines, set off from the safe harbour. Catch the trade winds in your sails. Explore. Dream. Discover." - Mark Twain

Of course it is easier to stick with what you have. I have met many people who have been stuck in relationships for years. It's no different if the relationship is between you and your company or two people.

You might have a job that works well enough to keep you ticking over. It is secure and comfortable. There's no need to break up and start afresh - but it's hardly an uplifting state of affairs.

Security at all kinds of levels is important to many of us. I was terrified when I closed the door leaving everything behind. I had bank loans and bills to pay like everyone else, but I had no option. If I wanted to become happy and alive again, I just had to turn to a brand new page and write a next chapter in life.

We are taught from a young age that we need to go to school and get good grades so we can find safe and secure jobs. But we are never taught how our grades are relevant to the world we live in. I remember asking my father why I had to spend my days in school when following him to work was so much more fun. He always said I needed something to fall back on.

Banks and other investors often ask budding entrepreneurs to run a SWOT (Strength, Weakness, Opportunity and Threat) analysis their business plan. This is to reassure the funding source that the applicant has a structure in place and some knowledge of the sector they are planning to enter.

I fully recommend that you carry out a similar exercise on yourself, whether you are an entrepreneur, owner, employee or student. Everything we do impacts on others and if we want to be part of something really successful and have fun at the same time, we'll save a lot of effort by focusing on what we really like.

What are your Strengths, Weaknesses, Opportunities and Threats for your personal success?
Below is a copy of a SWOT chart that I did for myself sometime ago. Do your own SWOT analysis using the SWOT chart found in the appendix section.

Swot:	s**W**ot:
I know myself well	Resolve problems head on, do not back away from them
I truly believe in my capacity to generate wealth	Do not always seek harmony in a group
I have enough knowledge and experience to take on any challenge	Do not let work take over my personal life where those I love most and my health should have priority
I am flexible, like new adventures and have financial freedom to try them	Don't let inner fears prevent me from following my heart

sw**O**t:	swo**T**:
View confrontations as an opportunity	Unwanted illness that I have no control over
Give the ones I love they want they need, not what I want to give	Market changes that are either unpredictable or uncontrolled
Find a new, more balanced way of life	Increase in competition within my field or sector

Knowing our own weaknesses and strengths, as well as having an awareness of future opportunities and risks, can also help us to identify those who can provide inspiration and support.

Eleanor Roosevelt said: "Do one thing every day that scares you." Imagine what would happen to your weaknesses if you did that!

When you learn to control your fears, to say no to people who pull you down and yes to those who lift you up, life's threats and weaknesses become a simple walk in the park, with opportunities and strengths shining through. All those excuses for postponing action are eliminated.

Our purpose and vision shape the choices we make, as well as our identity. We tend to live our lives as we believe they should be lived rather than how we would like them to be. I've interviewed so many mothers and women business managers who have limited expectations of what they can do. Not because they're bad at it but because of what is expected of them in being a good mother or wife. I've seen the same concerns when helping businesses grow from a period of stagnation. It's all about the choices we make and who and what we let ourselves be influenced by. Limitations are nothing but self-made barriers.

Instead of mixing with the kind of people who can inspire progress - in the same way as robber Willy Sutton wanted money so he went to banks - we tend to look at who we have around us and listen to them. We are governed by the rules and standards of our surroundings. A relationship break-up is always difficult whether it involves friends, family or colleagues. But if the people with whom you interact daily are not inspiring you to better things, are you capable enough to do it yourself?

Real freedom is so much more than having enough money to buy what you want. True, not having enough can prevent you from living how you'd like, but more isn't necessarily the answer. The problem is greater than that!
Your actions dictate your lifestyle, so instead of just seeing money as the answer to all your problems, ask yourself why you have these problems and how you got them.

While some may use lack of money or time as excuses for not being more successful, I suggest that boredom is a major factor, one which most of us forget or dare to admit to. When things are not going your way or you've lost your passion for work or in your relationship, excuses such as stress or not enough time sound much better than admitting you're bored.
Boredom is truly the number one enemy.
How likely is it that you'll make use of future opportunities if you are bored and fail to recognise them?

"What would life be if we had no courage to attempt anything?" - Vincent van Gogh

It can be all too easy to live to work rather than work to live; but life holds so much more. If you work 50 weeks a year, including late evenings and weekend working, you're more likely to go insane when you get your two-week holiday and want to see and do everything at once.

It's like taking someone to an all-you-can-eat buffet after they've been on a month-long liquid diet. Fingers crossed that they stay calm and only eat a tiny bit!

Life should not be all about the length of your annual holiday but what you do with the rest of the year. In my line of business I meet many people who think they are successful and important because they are in the office day and night. Being first in or the last to leave only counts if you are using that extra time to stay ahead of the game. If you think it's the hours that count rather than the final result, you are in trouble.

One particular friend of mine and I just cannot agree about holidays and work. He recently flew from America to Europe with his family for a two-week break. They spent two days in Milan, three in Rome, two in Paris and finished with three days in London. I appreciate that for some, visiting three different countries within a few days - not to mention the travel to each - can be relaxing, but I think the holiday itinerary my friend and his wife had put together was too busy for them to return from their break rested and full of energy.

Have you got the balance right?

Divide your life into sections, i.e. time, health, relationships etc and award points on a scale from 1-10 on how well you think you're doing. Look at the Balance of Life Chart provided in the appendix section. To get a good visual on your condition, the next step is to look at Circle of Life. Enter your marks into the circle. If you are in complete harmony, your "life" should resemble a circle. I still haven't met anyone with a perfect circle, you should see mine!! You'll find the Circle of Life Chart in the appendix section.

Although we can travel further than we ever have before, the time available to us to do it has grown shorter. True wealth is enjoyed by those who make time available so that they can fully experience the places they visit. The world's population is actually living longer, which means that we have extended the time we have to enjoy life compared to that of previous generations. However, so many of us are afraid of not being that oh-so-efficient multi-tasking whizz that we just keep running faster and faster to keep level with everybody else. No matter at what speed you live your life, make sure it's one that suits you.

Chapter 6

CREATING RELATIONSHIPS

"You can have everything you want in life if you just help enough people to get what they want." - Zig Ziglar

My head was aching and each breath was like a tiny blade cutting my throat. In total darkness I focused on following the light from my headlamp. My body was cold and I could hardly feel my fingers, but I didn't care - all the pain made me feel stronger at each step. I was climbing a steep slope that looked like it would go on forever so I kept telling myself to just keep putting one foot in front of the other. To my right the mountain precipice dropped off into the darkness and I could just make out the distant lights of the village of Chamonix. I was the last of a five-man team making its final ascent on the summit of Mt Blanc. We were 4 760m above sea level and, following five months of fierce training, I was nearing my goal. Suddenly the woman in front of me started stumbling drunkenly and, seconds later, dropped to the ground unconscious. As the rope holding us together snapped taught, I rammed my ice axe into the snow-covered wall, blocking what would have been a very ugly fall.

This was not happening, it couldn't be; not now, we were so close to the summit. We all knew that we were a team and no one was stronger than the weakest link. We all knew the routine, we had gone through everything in the cabin just a few hours earlier. It had all happened so fast.

I could only watch as the two men in front of Megan, the woman who had collapsed, simply cut themselves loose and continued their ascent without a backward look, their headlights growing weaker as they disappeared into the darkness. They seemed in a trance; nothing was going to stop them reaching the top.

I exchanged a look with our French guide Luc. We both knew what we had to do. A team member had been hit by altitude sickness and the only way to save her life was to act immediately. Knowing that I was about to embark on one of the hardest workouts of my life I helped Luc to get Megan on her feet and we started our slow decent.

Mt Blanc is often described as the roof of Europe and to conquer it is a dream shared by many, including me. But the challenges of climbing this legendary mountain should never be underestimated. Unfortunately, there are always people who think that climbing is easy as long as you are fit. Yes, you need to be reasonably fit to climb any mountain but there's more to it than that. As many as one third of all who try to climb Mont Blanc end up with some sort of injury such as frostbite, crampon wounds or problems associated with altitude. Most of these injuries could probably have been prevented if they had learned to climb and hike at lower levels first. This was the very first time Megan had tried any kind of climbing. Her gym instructor had led her to believe that all she needed was to train hard and everything would be a smooth walk uphill. That very same personal trainer that had now cut himself lose and just walked away and was somewhere closer to the summit than I was.

The mountain had been there for thousands of years and would always be there whether I had ascended its peak or not. What took three hours to climb now took five hours to descend. We couldn't stop; Megan was exhausted and had lost her sense of balance so we couldn't afford to make a single mistake.

I talked to her all the way down. I can't remember what I said but I knew I had to keep her focused on something other than the steep slopes on either side of us. "I'm too young to die," I kept telling myself. There were people who depended on me and I was going to doing everything, mentally and physically, I could to ensure we all got to safety.

Thankfully we made it to the village. I knew Megan was more than grateful, but there was no need for words. For me it was the rule of the game; you come as a team and you leave as one. Yes, I was disappointed I hadn't reached the summit but, more importantly, I was proud of myself ignoring my own ego to reach out to someone in greater need.

I knew now that I had found the inner strength that I had been seeking. The fact that I'd been able to put Megan's needs before my own gave me an inner peace and I realised that the harmony of my mind and soul, destroyed by my divorce a few months earlier, had been restored. Finally I felt healed, complete and ready to both love and to be loved again.

I could not even be angry with the two men when they returned from the mountain the next afternoon as if nothing had happened. I just felt sorry for them.

There are plenty of tricks and tactics for achieving a one-off success, but that success can be short-lived and can have a long-term destructive influence. The two who kept going after Megan collapsed owned a gym and were personal trainers. Reaching the top of Mt Blanc earned them five minutes of fame in their local newspaper, but then the story of our rescue effort emerged. They may have reached the top but the impact of their actions, driven by their ambition, was long lasting and impacted badly on their business.

"Progress is impossible without change and those who cannot change their minds cannot change anything"
- George Bernard Shaw

In the world of business, regardless of how well you know your own products or services, you will need to understand the systems and processes as well as have a broad understanding of the underlying business issues and goals of your potential client. Without these insights you cannot fully consider how your products and services will meet your potential clients' needs, nor will you be able to tell them why they should buy from you.

One way to achieve this, and to create stronger connections, is to mirror other people. On Mt Blanc for example, if the gym instructors had paid more attention to Megan and mirrored her behaviour and actions during the ascent, they would have most likely sensed that everything was not as it should be.

Mirroring is not the same as copying. Mirroring means that you look at the behaviour people exhibit in different situations and make them feel a connection. So if you meet people that speak quietly, lower your voice. Such techniques enable you to recognise personality traits - an amiable individual or someone of a more technical bent - and adjust how you present a product, service or yourself accordingly.

It's a process that requires a great deal of social skill, as well as the need to put your own egotistical wants aside, to focus on the person in front of you.

However social skills get people talking. All about me, me, me is boring - start asking questions and people will remember you for being the one interested in them. Human beings are social creatures who love hanging out with like-minded people.

"One day you will wake up and there wont be any more time to do the things you've always wanted. Do it now!" - Paulo Coelho

Take golf. It has been said that many business deals are made on the golf course. I don't know if there are statistics to prove that the likelihood of making a deal is higher at the golf course than at a bar, however, I do know that golf is a sport that most people can learn to play and, most importantly, play together regardless of their gender, age or physical condition.

That means it opens up some common ground which can create a base for trust. We all feel more at ease with people who are like us and therefore more business deals are made. I once coached a manager in Italy who was the only woman on the board of an international company and who felt her views at meetings were not taken as seriously by her colleagues. When I asked her if they treated her differently in any other way, she said no. I asked her if she was excluded from any of the group activities or invitations to events; she said no. The more I talked to her I realised that she had turned down every invitation board members had received from their clients in the last five years as she just wasn't interested in playing golf, attending Formula 1 racing events or car shows.

I pointed out that if she wanted to be part of the group she also sometimes had to do what the majority wanted and, thus, find some common ground with her colleagues outside the boardroom.

I am not suggesting that being the only woman on a company board is easy, but knowing that most of the key decisions due to made in a meeting have already been taken away from the boardroom only underlines how crucial it is to ensure that you have been part of that process through finding some common ground with the others before entering that room. The principle's the same when working with any group be it a college, or of clients or board members.

When we're seeking to build personal relationships, finding common ground is the first thing we do when looking for dating opportunities, so it's not like we don't know how to do it. Business is no different. The more we spend time with each other the more we learn how we function together and the more fun we have, making it easier to get the work done.

"Love is a force more formidable than any other. It is invisible – it cannot be seen or measured, yet it is powerful enough to transform you in a moment and offer you more joy than any material possession could."
- Barbara D'angelis

I remember a job interview I had at Vodafone during my time at University. It was one of the greatest conversations I ever had and I will always remember it because it proved to me at a very young age that I should just be who I am. I spotted a poster of someone skiing down Mt Blanc. Being a passionate skier myself I recognised the image and, without thinking, started talking about how great the picture was. The interview turned into an enthusiastic chat in which we talked about skiing and different resorts around the world and one hour turned into two or three. The job was never mentioned, but when we finally finished, the manager just asked me to see his assistant so I could sign the employment contract before I left and to start as soon as I felt like it.

Before you judge a group of people or make a statement of fact based on gender, age, business group or anything else, take a minute to consider what the common ground between its members might be. You need to do this if you wish to be a part of this group, and if it's one you have to work with you must learn to communicate in a way that the members understand and are comfortable with. Using different languages is seldom just an exchange of words, it tends to include a communication between different cultures.

If you want to have a great relationship in your personal business life, then let go of your ego. Be aware of your clients, employees, colleagues, and partner - listen to them. Focus on the needs and interests of others. But always remember, giving people what they want does not necessary mean to give it for free.

Chapter 7

KEEP YOUR EYES ON THE HORIZON

"You can accomplish anything in life as long as you do not care about who gets the honour for it." - Harry S. Truman

I was sitting at the bar at the Millenium Hotel in Kensington, London when Hans, a consultant from Stockholm, called me. We had met a few times through a mutual client. His son had just contracted flu and he needed to be at a meeting in the Scandinavian mountains the very next evening. I was traveling back home after a great conference in London and as I had no plans, I agreed to take his place. If I found the project interesting I could take over. I promptly booked a flight ticket and an hour long taxi trip to a small ski resort with just 200 inhabitants. I arrived in a trench coat and high heels. Talk about out of place!

But this meeting ended up in me gaining new friends for life and a challenging mission for the coming year.

I was once given the opportunity to take on a failing company and turn its fortunes around. I guess most people would have turned their backs on such an enormous challenge - but then I'm not like most people. When others say something is impossible I like to prove them wrong. I prefer to see it as problem that is a bit harder to solve. In this instance I was tackling a business which had been operating successfully for so many years that the staff had forgotten to put the customers first.

When business is good, it's so easy to become complacent and forget where the money that pays your salary comes from. Good business practice begins and ends with the customer as the central focus of attention. Unfortunately there are company owners and managers who do lose touch with their clients' needs, usually when business couldn't be better. This loss of focus is often the first warning sign that damage is being inflicted upon an organisation.

The same thing can happen to us as individuals. Whether or not we want to admit it, we're influenced by those within our social groups, so if we want to improve ourselves we have to associate with people exhibiting the same successful personality traits and characteristics that we are looking for.

The principle is no different when it comes to climbing the career ladder. They might not be aware of it, but your employers and potential employers will subconsciously look for people who remind them of themselves. That process might not always work in a company's best interests, but it is just the way we humans work. That's why so many businesses deals or job appointments are made at social events, such as at the golf course or a party. Mixing with like-minded people fosters a sense of security.

Think about those customers who you really want to attract. How can you find out what they want from you?

You will probably need to ask questions that aren't too different to the ones I suggested you ask yourself at the beginning of this book. At the end it all comes down to knowing what they want and/or need and how you can deliver it!

What do they get if they do business with you?
Why should they deal with you rather than anyone else?
These wants and needs are not constant though, they are in a constant state of flux and are unlikely to remain static for long. Business never stands still, the faster it moves, the more often you will need to ask questions.

The best way to get ahead is to create a bond with your clients so that they are comfortable telling you what they want. It's exactly the same if you are an employee; building a bond with your manager or board of directors will give you insight into what they are looking for from you. You can never assume what the other party wants, whether it be your partner, a potential employer or client, but it is your job to find out, simple as that. It's your responsibility to discover why people are coming to you and what they expect you to do for them. To achieve this successfully you need to put their needs before your own.

Nowadays people don't only look for the fastest or easiest option, they usually want what gives them the best value for money, no matter what the price is. You cannot count on loyalty if you didn't provide value for money with a previous purchase.

While the internet and social media enable us to showcase positive images of ourselves, our services and products, they are just as powerful at highlighting negatives, which can spread across the globe in an instant. That's why creating relationships that can withstand challenging situations is more important than ever.

"We all have the same boss, the customer, and he can fire us any time he wants by deciding to buy somewhere else."
- Sam Walton, the founder of American multi-national retail corporation Wal-Mart. [3]

A satisfied customer is far easier to sell to than a new customer. A referral from a satisfied customer will give you greater success than a cold call. So how do you create a bond with people you've never met?

Do your research, ask pertinent questions and be persistent; they may not come round at first but if you can make them understand that you are genuine, there's every likelihood that they will eventually respond positively. Remember, your key message is that your business can help them. Take time to listen to their needs and change your products and services accordingly before they start shopping elsewhere. Your customers will help you to stay one step ahead of the game if you allow them to.

Many people in a competitive market make the mistake of dismissing the competition. Smart business folk, however, not only respect successful competitors, they study and learn from them. Do not equate studying with copying though. Copying is a certain recipe for disaster. You want to be slightly ahead of

---

[3] Sam Walton, Made in America

the pack, not spending all your resources looking at what everybody else is doing.

The secret to company growth is being able to attract a steady stream of new clients while keeping existing ones. Remember that the fastest and most secure way to build a successful business is to keep improving a successful product or service. Sometimes an idea only needs tweaking a tiny amount to be able to capture substantial new shares of the market.

Look at the iPhone, for example. Apple first released the iPhone 3 which was then followed by the iPhone 4, 4s, iPhone 5 and 5s and so on. There's not actually a great difference between each successive version, but by just making a few changes and upgrading some functions Apple created demand from all those end users wanting to own the latest model and, thus, boosted sales.

"A friendship founded on business is better than a business founded on friendship." - John D. Rockefeller

Have you lost some of your clients?

It costs a fortune to acquire a new customer but almost nothing to regain an old one. All you need to do to create repeat business is to make them an offer they can't refuse or just get in touch with them to show them that you care and genuinely want to know how they are doing.

I recently met up with an old friend, Kevin, at an event in California, USA and he started to confide all his business worries to me. Although he was about twice my age, I found myself in the bizarre position of being asked for some business advice. He was not a paying client but a friend asking for some guidance. Now, while I will, happily share my thoughts and experiences, I'm always very careful not to specifically tell people what to do, particularly if friends are involved. I don't want to build my businesses based on friendships. I also know that whatever I say is unlikely to have any real effect unless the recipient is ready to act upon my advice and make changes.

Kevin, who owned a large IT company on America's west coast, told me he'd noticed that in the last two years he'd made less money than he had done ten years ago when he started the business.
I started asking some pretty simple questions, such as how many repeat clients he had, how many new jobs were via referrals from current clients and how often he would call clients to see how things were. Kevin went quiet for a minute before admitting that he had never once called a client after a job was finished, and neither had his employees.

Sadly, he's not the only one to never follow up after a job is completed. In the financial services industry it is common practice to ask for and receive referrals as clients reap benefits from our services. It is something that can so easily be done by other companies, but seldom is.

I have worked with many IT businesses which provide millions of dollars-worth of solutions to customers and, like Kevin, they never make follow-up calls. Yet Kevin had helped major movie studios, hotel chains and car manufacturers, sectors that all needed upgrades at some point in time.

Any financial adviser would think you insane if you acquired one client while they were in college and then never contacted them when they got married, had children or started thinking about retirement, second houses etc. We humans need different advice as we go through life, whether it be from doctors, trainers or financial advisors.

Companies are no different and if you spend time building a bond at the outset of a new relationship, you could gain a client for life.

I asked Kevin to call the ten clients he had had the most fun working with as I wanted him to focus on them rather than those who had generated the most income for his company. We know that we do a better job when we have more fun and I wanted him to be passionate enough to re-establish a relationship with those clients. I wanted him to care about them and their problems in order to build a base for a joint business future.

Three months later he called me to say his business had performed better in the last quarter than the previous year. Although he thanked me and offered to pay me back in some way, I asked him to "pay it forward". I prefer to share with others and to have people share with me. This, I believe, helps the world we live in become just a little bit better.

We need entrepreneurs who can help each other grow and keep the economy buoyant, even through tough times. Great business relationships are based on more than the next purchase or selling opportunity. By delivering the same high quality service to a client, no matter the size of the order, you create a bond that encompasses empathy and understanding.

Everyone can be a great manager or salesperson during the good times but it's when you are faced with a real challenge that your skills are truly tested.
If your clients' orders are on the decline, ask yourself why. Is it because they're not satisfied with the service you provide or can they no longer afford you?
Why not create a solution to that will help them and result in them retaining your services? Keep your head high, leave your ego behind and concentrate on your client's needs.

Chapter 8

STEPPING OUT OF YOUR COMFORT ZONE

"People take different roads seeking fulfilment and happiness. Just because they're not on your road doesn't mean they've got lost." - Dalai Lama

I meet people every now and then who just cannot understand why someone like myself would give up a high paying job in vibrant bustling cities like Tokyo or Singapore to live in the rural tranquility of Scandinavia. It is not always easy to explain why we choose the paths we do, but the journey to fulfilment and happiness is different for everyone. For me it is to be able to travel around the globe. This hunger has taken me from that dreaming eight year-old with a terrible drawing, standing in front of a laughing class, to someone with the world as her playground. If money had been everything to me I never would have travelled to far flung places - but I probably would have been bored and unfulfilled.

I've always just grabbed things. I may not have always made the right move, but you get just one shot and that's why I've always thrown myself to into life's next adventure with gratitude and humility.

Charlie Chaplin once said: *"Life can be wonderful if you're not afraid of it. All it takes is courage, imagination ... and a little dough."*

Off course he was right in that having a little bit of money alleviates the fear of not being able to pay the bills or put food on the table. However, that same fear can also hold you back - you're much more motivated if you don't have anything. Remember, the best goals are the ones you create yourself and by stepping out of your comfort zone you can enjoy experiences that would never happen in your safe, but probably unexciting, place.

Taking your business or life onto the world stage is a great way of leaving those comfort zones.
Even those working at a global level are constantly surprised at the varying behaviours of different cultures.
We tend to believe that humans are the same deep inside, but that's not really the case and so if, while abroad, we make decisions based on how we operate at home, the chances are we'll make some very bad ones. The same applies if you're dealing with international investors on your home turf. They may recognise the same business opportunity as you but don't assume they are thinking about it in same way as you or that they understand how business is conducted in your country.

Make sure you get first-hand information about a country and its business methods and don't assume anything, including relying on books which may have been based on second or third-hand knowledge.

"One can choose to go back toward safety or forward toward growth. Growth must be chosen again and again; fear must be overcome again and again."
- Abraham Maslow

Communicating with other cultures can be challenging; it may sometimes feel impossible. And yet, just when nothing appears to be making sense, this is often when you will have a breakthrough. You've let your fear go and reached that state of mind where you just don't care about making a fool of yourself. This will improve your ability to facilitate successful communication between different cultures, opening new doors both in life and in business.

Cross-cultural differences do not only cover language, food or ways of dress, but also non-verbal behaviours, religious beliefs, manners, customs, forms of address, body language or gestures, to name but a few. Knowing the language is not the same as knowing the culture.

Most international organisations are aware of the potential damage misunderstandings can cause around the globe. However, in our multi-cultural societies, such challenges can be faced much closer to home than you might think.

Misunderstandings or ignorance about a certain behaviour can cause stress, followed by dissatisfaction with a product, service or business dealings. I've worked with people who have refused to take an international phone call or ignore emails so that they don't have to communicate with someone from a different country.

I have been a foreigner in another country for half my life, I love learning new things. It's great when the task of cultural communication becomes a challenge and not a barrier. To be successful at an international level, one needs to understand how cultural factors influence business methods and implement strategies that can successfully target that particular group.

Different cultures and subcultures are everywhere and we simply need to adapt. Getting stressed by not understanding won't get you anywhere. Relax and enjoy opportunity of learning something new.

"We create stress for ourselves because you feel like you have to do it. You have to. I don't feel that anymore."
- Oprah Winfrey

Sometimes we overlook certain groups as potential clients because communicating with them would force us to step outside our comfort zones.

When I was involved in reviving the business mentioned in chapter 7, I looked at who its previous partners were and found that some stood out more than others. I decided to call them and, after thanking them for their business, asked what they needed us to do to improve our service. They told me greater flexibility and more cost-effective pricing. I made sure that this was put into effect and demand increased.

The only thing that I had done differently to anyone else before me was to step out of the company comfort zone and start asking questions. I was able to take an outside perspective, look at its aims and ask why it even existed in the first place and why people did business with it.

Take a minute to think about why your specific culture is unique. The more you know about your own background, the easier it is to spot the differences in others.

The world today is a huge melting pot of different peoples and cultures. It's too easy to say that when moving to another country, either to work or live, everyone should adjust to its way of life. It doesn't work that way. We may have to adapt to a certain degree but our original cultural roots will always remain. If we want be successful at selling ideas, services or products, the best and quickest way is to put potential customers or the needs of the business first.

I have already talked about the success you can have by mirroring people and if you only remember two points from this chapter it should be:
1. Always mirror your host, foreign business partner or market.
2. Show a humble understanding towards a new culture.

If you think about it, it's not that different from meeting a new partner. You go that little bit further and embrace the task of getting to know someone new.
If you've met someone you like, you'll probably do just about anything to make sure they pick you, so why not make that extra effort in a business setting? There is no such thing as the best culture or the best country - even though we sometimes like to see it that way. There are only values with which you may or may not associate yourself.

Look outwards from the inside. An organisation is never better than the people who are at its heart – the employees. And if they are not motivated, they won't perform with passion. This will result in products not being delivered in time, poor service and worsening company figures. This is what had happened with the company I assisted. The employees had been there for so long they couldn't separate the needs of the business with their own needs. One lady, for example, contacted her son whenever maintenance was required at any of the firm's properties. She never considered the rates offered by other firms which could have meant reduced costs for the company.

Being open to any eventuality is actually the hard part of international business success.

Studying for my MBA at Waseda University, in Tokyo, my blonde hair and British accent meant I stood out. Just as well blending in never was an option for me - I wouldn't have succeeded no matter how hard I tried. Despite the amount of work I put into my tan, I was always the pale skinned one from the Viking country.

One night after school, I was approached by Sunny, a Korean girl. I had observed my Korean classmates for some time and had noticed how they tended to stick together, not really associating with the others. Coming so close that I had to consciously try not to take a step back, Sunny invited me to join her and a group of friends for dinner.

I accepted the invitation but when she took my hand and, accompanied by her friends, began leading me through the maze of alleys making up Tokyo's Korean quarter, I couldn't have felt more uncomfortable. It crossed my mind that no one would miss me at all if I disappeared and while I very much wanted to let go of her hand, I was also afraid of offending her, so I just kept telling myself that we would soon reach our destination.

I had always thought of myself as someone with a very global perspective who was open to all different cultures, but even I was now a bit uneasy having been taken by out of my comfort zone by this surprise invitation.

Of course we did get there and I had a wonderful time but as we went seemingly in circles around the maze-like streets, I told myself I was still among my classmates who were actually great people, and focused on the generosity of being invited into a group that didn't normally let in foreigners.

A month later I was invited to a business event in Seoul and soon thereafter was flying into the South Korea capital on a monthly basis to seek new clients. None of that would have been possible if I hadn't had that invitation from Sunny prompting me to an even higher appreciation and acceptance of a new culture and experience. Even the most experienced traveller can be faced with difficult and demanding cross-cultural encounters, but if you remain open to all eventualities, and step out your comfort zone, you will be rewarded, sometimes in the most unexpected ways.

Abraham Lincoln summed it up very well. *"Strangers are like friends you still haven't met."* I think those words are more important than ever to remember in today's global society. You never know where your new clients may come from.

By contrast, the seasoned business traveller can fall victim to international blindness. Too much travelling may result in different countries and cultures becoming a blur. For example, someone travelling from North America would find it very easy to regard Europe as one huge, borderless market. However treating it as such, whether it's in marketing, sales or business negotiations, will guarantee failure for the simple reason that each country making up the continent has its own cultural traditions, values and language.

There is also a variety of religious and political systems, some of which have been closed to foreign influences for many years, and while certain countries have been engaged in warfare there are others, like my own country Sweden, who haven't been involved in a conflict for over 200 years!

Chapter 9

LIFE - THE GREAT ROLLER COASTER

"It's not what you say out of your mouth that determines your life, it's what you whisper to yourself that has the most power." - Robert T. Kiyosaki

I was on the phone with Carrie, my business coach, looking back over the past year. Somehow I had managed to get married and file for divorce. I had moved, bought a second home, a new car, had ten weeks' holiday and met tons of great new people and some interesting clients.

I was really annoyed because I hadn't signed a contract with a client earlier, but Carrie asked me to put aside what I had not achieved that morning and focus on everything I had done during the year instead.

I had made an enormous journey in those twelve months, more, in fact, than some do in a lifetime, but I had got caught up in what I had not done during that one morning.

Progress brings us happiness but if we've given ourselves a lengthy list of 'to-dos', or goals which can be achieved within a day or two, it will be hard to measure any progress at all and we'll end up feeling under pressure instead. That very pressure will then create stress which makes us worry about every conceivable setback, no matter how small. It prevents us from moving forward.

As I've mentioned before, it's often the steps we take to towards our goals which are more important than the goals themselves.

You might well encounter problems along the way, but having to solve them is certainly beneficial to one's personal development. This could apply, as in my case, to the process of buying a new home, which was of far greater use than my ultimate goal: actual home ownership.

Remember, even if nothing is as easy as we anticipate, never give up. Keep moving and you WILL see progress.

Keep tabs on your success by regularly referring back to that list of goals I urged to you write down at the beginning of this book.

I strongly recommend that you identify stepping stones towards your final goal, like a company breaking its annual financial objective into quarterly targets. Going faster is not always the best solution because if you make mistakes, it'll take you even longer to get back on track.

Here's an example.

You want to run the New York Marathon so you will need enough physical strength to complete it and enough financial strength to fund your travel to the Big Apple. Instead of focusing on getting fit for the entire distance, set up some markers, or signposts, such as each time you break your own speed record, or every time you smash through a 10km milestone.

Financially, set your signposts at points nearing the total amount you need to raise. If you only focus on the marathon as a whole your training will become very tough. By celebrating every time you pass a marker, the whole journey towards your ultimate goal will be much more fun.

The same principle applies to other things in life. No matter how well-defined your goals are, there will always be times when you feel a bit down or things are tough. That's when having smaller goals to achieve really becomes important.

At one point, things were going so fast for me that I forgot those reality checks. And then cold, hard reality hit on that afternoon when I found myself under the Singapore sun on the Ritz Hotel terrace with Paul.

I was one of the youngest and most successful financial advisers, with a gift of getting deals sealed. I had started my journey in Japan, travelled in and out of Monaco, China, Korea and now Singapore. I needed just five more years of working like this and living out of a suitcase, then I could retire. At least that was my plan.

But now I realised that I was mainly surrounded by people who were far older than me and still looking for the next big deal. I remembered how happy I had been when I received the pay cheque from my first financial deal back in Tokyo - $27,619. I'd never earned that much before and, at the time, it felt as though I was walking on clouds. Two years had passed since then and I now wouldn't consider taking on anything that brought me less than $100,000. But time spent travelling on business trips around the islands of Malaysia had given me time to think about who I was and what mattered the most in life.

Paul, despite his high-powered financial career, remained at heart a simple man and he had seen right through me.
He leaned forward, looked deep into my eyes and said: "Johanna, finance has found you and you are great at what you do. In fact you are flying higher than most only ever dream of. I know who you are, I know what you can do, now it is time for you to decide who you want to be."

His words, like knives, pierced my heart. I knew he was right. For eight months I had been living a dream, but the dream wasn't mine. I had been living life in the fast lane but I had forgotten everything I had learned from all those powerful and successful men and women on my way up. I had been so focused on aiming high financially.

"It's not whether you get knocked down, it's whether you get up." - Vince Lombardi

I had come to realise that real wealth was happiness, something that no money could buy. Going after financial reward had become boring and I'd lost all passion for it.

If I was not happy, what was I?

If you're not happy with the person you are, any journey towards your goals will be far more difficult. We cannot change the past but we can change the future. I knew I wanted mine to be filled with personal fulfilment and adventures.

After my drink with Paul I headed to the hotel room that had been my home for the last few months and packed my bags, arranging for all but one duffel bag to be shipped to my parents in Sweden.

With that one lightly packed bag I headed off towards the Malaysian Islands, starting on the east side with Tioman, and told myself I wouldn't return to Singapore or leave the region until I had found my true self again.

The first things I questioned were my financial goals - if I didn't have time to do anything but work, why did I need them? I did get time off, but it was tiny in comparison to the hours I put in at the office. It seemed my job owned me; I had no control over what time I started or when my working day would finish. I didn't know what the following week held in store or even what country I would visit next. This enormous feeling of helplessness was all related to a financial number that I was chasing without knowing why.

Paul made me face the stark truth that I had gone off course. This enabled me to realise that wealth is not a number on a bank statement. It's a state of mind which only we can create. The real winners aren't the ones who reap rich financial rewards when the market's booming, they're the ones who lose very little when things take a turn for the worse.

Earlier I talked about the importance of quality relationships and how they matter in the world of investments. It's easy to forget that when business is booming, but you must stay focused and have a back-up plan ready for when the inevitable downturn comes.

I used to be brilliant at telling clients about the benefits of 'passive incomes', but the truth is there's no such thing. You will never gain anything by being passive, financially or personally. You have to look after things and if you don't, you will lose them.

During my great roller coaster ride of a turbulent year, I realised that money, and relationships were the same: if you take care of them and treat them well, they will repay you dividends.

TV personality Oprah Winfrey, who has been voted the most influential woman in the world and one of America's richest people says: *"Don't worry about being successful but work toward being significant and the success will naturally follow."*

Clearly stating your goals will help you keep your head high and vision clear through stormy times. Don't let mainstream thinking deter you from your course. A good way of staying focused is to create a 'vision board'; a collage of images that symbolises your goals and maintains your motivation. Let it be like a treasure map of your dreams, put up pictures of anything that you're passionate about!

Vision boards work just as well for companies and organisations as for individuals. I used one when I successfully transformed the fortunes of a travel company's reservations department.

Now the staff have a constant visual reminder of where the company wants to be and it helps them focus on the end product as well as meeting every customer's individual requirement.

Try using a vision board yourself; an example is provided in the appendix section at the end of the book.

In business, a market can change out of all recognition within hours and without warning and that's why companies need to be able to react appropriately, even it if means leaving their comfort zone. Major events can have a profound affect on the business sector, there are many examples to choose from.

Within the airline industry it is widely recognised that the tragic events of September 11, when as a result, every flight leaving to, from and within the USA was grounded, represents a watershed in how the airlines operated.

Even if there were signs of what was to come before the change, the industry was primarily occupied with transferring passengers from A to B, creating strategic alliances so that passengers could fly across the world within one network and get frequent flyer miles. Directly after 9/11, airlines began to include hotels, car rentals, airport transfer and shopping - a more complete experience of travel and lifestyle.

There will be times when we too, as people, are thrown off course by a major incident or event that we could never have anticipated. Adapting to events on a personal level is not always as easy as it is for a business, but if we surround ourselves with positive people who can inspire us to go forward, it all becomes much easier.

Remember, progress is impossible without change and those who find change a problem will cause you problems! When I started working at the travel company, everybody was happy because I was bringing changes they wanted. I was the sales and marketing expert who would save the company. However when I started explaining what I needed from them to achieve the company's goals they began to resist me. They just couldn't understand that changing the course of the business also meant changing the way they did things. Unfortunately, the staff had all become very good at talking about each other but really bad at talking to each other. They had become detached from the business.

Life is a roller coaster and more often than not we focus on the things that are just in front of us instead taking a more panoramic view. Adopting a wider vision will enable you to see opportunities for yourself and for your business.
The world is in constant motion and will keep moving whether you do or not.

You only give up when you stop trying!

Chapter 10

ROLL THE DICE

"Your time is limited. Don't waste it living someone else's life. Don't be trapped by dogma, which is living with the results of other people's thinking. Don't let the noise of others' opinion drown out your own inner voice. Most important, have the courage to follow your heart and intuition. They somehow already know what you truly want to become. Everything else is secondary." - Steve Jobs

There can come a time in life when taking a new direction makes sense even though just the thought of all that could go wrong is quite frightening.

I have been extremely lucky, or daft - call it what you want - and since a child, have yearned for adventure. I was once asked by a company president where I would want to live within five years. I could only reply that although I had absolutely no idea, I did know what my life would look like and what I'd be doing. My vision boards and lists with objectives have always been very specific when it comes to time but never with places. I truly feel just at home in a small mountain resort in Scandinavia as I do in the heart of Tokyo or on the beaches of the French Riviera. Yes, I've made some wrong decisions, but I made them from the heart and they have led me on a remarkable road of discovery, supplying me with memories I will treasure as long as I live.

The stories of great companies do not differ greatly than those of great lives or love affairs. They've all featured an element of risk, even if it has been a calculated risk.

You cannot play with small stakes and expect to reap rich rewards. If you really love someone you have to invest time and passion, putting that person's needs before yours, not because you have to but because you want to.

The same applies to any business. If you put the company's needs first your chances of success are far greater than if you try to use the company to satisfy your requirements. Luxembourg hedge fund manager Véronique (see chapter 3) would come in a bit earlier to work or stay an hour later because she wanted to stand out at what she did. But she also brought a substantial amount of income into the companies she worked for and enjoyed a tremendous career. She taught me not to be afraid of walking away from a well-paid opportunity that didn't actually do anything for more me than boosting my bank balance.

Taking a calculated business risk also means passing up opportunities which may have great financial potential but are not in line with company values. Certainly, fear shouldn't stop us from taking advantage of available opportunities but we need to able to say no to those that instinctively don't feel right.

When the opportunity came up to work in Japan and later Singapore, the 'what ifs' never crossed my mind. I instinctively felt they were good moves and just went with them. If I had thought things through when Paul asked me to join his finance firm, any fears of failure could have made me say no. After all, I was doing very well in marketing - what did I know about finance?

So, even though I have never been one to shy away from a new opportunity, I have had to learn how to say no!

This is often a problem of knowing your real value. It's very easy to say yes to every new business project, but while that is definitely going to give you more work, it won't necessarily bring in more money or a profit.
'Working smart' is just as much about taking on contracts that feel right as it is as refusing those that you don't feel will work for you, even if the money's good.

But sometimes you just need to roll the dice and rely on your inner instincts

In chapter 7 and 8 I recalled how I was head-hunted to revive the fortunes of a company which had fallen on difficult times.

The company and the tourism sector in which it operated had been expanding for so many years that staff and management had become complacent. They spent more time talking amongst themselves than their clients. I remember their surprised response when I declared the first rule at the reservations department. Answer all calls! They were so tired of bookings that they had stopped answering calls when it was time for a coffee break (which became longer and longer!). The problem was the employees' attitude towards work. They had misinterpreted the growth in their sector as a result of them doing a great job. When the economy reversed they blamed it on everything else but never focused on what they could do to enhance bookings. The employees had let themselves become the focus of attention rather than the market and they were so attached to their own habits that any other work practices were intimidating. New markets identified by the board of directors were regarded with huge suspicion.

Although I did turn the company around I didn't manage to change the attitudes of everyone working there. They didn't mind change, just as long as it was someone else who had to do it! I took on the challenge, not because of the salary, but because the investors and owners shared my passion for the business they worked in - skiing, biking and other outdoor activities. From our very first meeting I thought the people would be a great group to work with and since people like to hangout with like-minded people it was hard to refuse this challenging opportunity.

Is grasping an opportunity guided only by your instinct and passion really as easy as I make it sound?
Well, if you follow my guidelines and write down your goals and why you really want them, then yes it is!

As a coach I have met many people who have identified their goals, know why they want to reach them and what they need to do in order to achieve them. But they have then been prevented from moving forward by their financial security fears.

Worry about financial risk is often what that gets in the way of great ideas. I always help my clients identify their financial strengths in order for them to feel more confident. A person's financial strength is influenced by who they are and what lifestyle they have.

Some feel secure knowing that they have money for the week, others need to know that there will be enough for the next year or longer. There is no right kind of security; there is only the one with which you feel comfortable. One that will allow you to sleep well at night and take the calculated risks needed to go forward.

So how do you work out what your level of financial security is?

There are many ways but I've found the simplest and easiest way for my clients is to total all their monthly living expenses, including house, car, clothes, food, etc, and then work out what they could cut back on and still be able to live comfortably. We also identify what minimum income is necessary to ensure financial security.

If you wish to do this exercise yourself look at my listed examples below. What you include will depend on your personal circumstances: whether you have children, your marital status, if you are living with someone and so on. You will need to work out how much you need to cover your living expenses in a worst-case scenario

1. Mortgage/rent	$ 2,000
2. Food	$ 500
3. Utilities	$ 500
4. Transport	$ 500
5. Taxes	$ 500
6. School fees	$ 200
7. Unexpected extras	$ 200
Monthly income necessary for security	$ 4,400

This client aimed at earning $7,000 a month which meant a surplus of $2,600.

Suddenly that income didn't seem too unattainable which inspired confidence. The next step is to work out how many months of saving is needed to build up a lump sum which can be kept for rainy days.

If your monthly salary is lower than the figure you just calculated, it's most likely that you're living on credit and your financial security is already maxed out. It's time for you to look at your costs and see which of them you can do something about.

The secret to many millionaires and billionaires' fortunes is that they spend less then they earn. It is as simple as that and yet so many people find it hard to follow. You are the source of your future and you have to be in control of your own financial security before you can start thinking about the finances of your business.

Sadly, far more people globally than we'd like to believe already live far beyond their means. That's why a shift in the market or the collapse of a major company, such as that of

Lehman Brothers in 2008, can have such an enormous effect on the world's economy.

Earlier I pointed out how important it is not to let your life be dictated by your surroundings. This is just as important when creating your own financial strength.

IKEA founder Ingvar Kamprad, one of the world's richest people, has said: *"Becoming rich is not about the large incomes it's about the small expenses"*[4].

This should be one of the most fundamental aspects of business to understand, but the truth is that success does not suddenly fall upon us, it accumulates over time.

Most of us find it easier to spend more the more we get and while there's nothing wrong with buying things we like, it has to be in relation to what we earn and that is not always the case.

Take professional athletes for example, many of who have been known to find themselves broke no more than five years after their high-paying careers have ended. Most talented athletes sign contracts when they are young and, let's face it, who wouldn't when, aged about 18, you're presented with the opportunity of "working" for 10 years, retiring at 30 and being financially set for life?

---

[4] http://www.forbes.com/profile/ingvar-kamprad

Sadly, few at such a young age have any financial discipline and as *Broke*, a US TV documentary[5] depicted, most pro athletes are completely broke less than 10 years following retirement.

How can someone earning millions of dollars lose it all so quickly? If you think about it, many young people have not yet learned how handle financial matters; they remain very much in the hands of their parents. And if you don't know how to legitimately make a million dollars, you will only have a vague idea of how to keep a million dollars.

Build up your own financial reserve as children build a snowman. You start with a tiny little snowball that you slowly and carefully roll along the ground so that it picks up more snow and gradually gets bigger and bigger. Sooner or later you reach that point where that little snowball has become so big that it just rolls by itself.

When you are earning money and feeling great, it is hard to think about that day when you have to start rolling the snowman all over again. It is important to know your financial strength so that you can still feel comfortable during the days when a job or business deal doesn't go as planed. Knowing how long you can last without needing to work can be a great way of measuring your own financial wealth.

---

[5] http://bleacherreport.com/articles/1356918-espns-broke-barely-scratched-the-surface-of-athlete-bankruptcy-discussion
20140331

Throughout the world healthy eating, fresh water, good healthcare or education all have to be paid for. Money also influences our relationships with friends and family. There will always be factors outside our control when it comes to assessing our financial strength, but it is we ourselves who have the ultimate control. Take a minute and think about what you could do differently if you had the funds, and then think again about why you are not doing anything about it. If you have your goals ready and you know why you want to reach them, it shouldn't be so hard to get there.

"Don't ask what the world needs. Ask what makes you come alive and go do it. Because what the world needs is people who have come alive." - H. Thurman

Wealth is a psychological state of mind. Of course, having money is a very important part of being able to choose where and how you want to live. But it is crucial to make the distinction between wealth and riches.

Anyone who has a lot of money can be rich but in order to have real wealth, one has to feel truly happy within oneself. To accomplish this you need to fully engage with the people you meet at work and in your personal life and with your inner self. It's all about triggering feelings. When you take that big step forward, to roll that dice, stay focused, let the energy flow and the passion that you generate will trigger inner strength. Convincing sceptical clients is so much easier if you can share your passion, affecting them in such a positive way that they, in turn, are inspired and energised to respond.

At a business seminar in London I once met a man from Belgium who held a high-ranking position within the European Parliament. He told me of his dream to run a juice bar on the coast of Belgium and to teach youngsters how to surf. He then asked me to put together a sales and marketing strategy for his idea.

The work would have been well paid and it was a good excuse for me to visit Brussels but I just couldn't detect any passion from him about what he wanted to do. He described his ambition in a very factual and bland way; his body language didn't become animated and he never conjured up any vivid images for me.

I turned down the job. I'm still in contact with him but, two years on, he still works at the same office, still lives in the same city house, still has no time to spend at the beach and he's still dreaming about opening that juice bar.

It's extremely important to work with people that like to have fun and enjoy what they are doing. If I do not feel their passion when they talk, I will not work with them.
My brother once asked me to help his friend Anders who was winning heavily by playing internet poker but had been smart enough to put all the money into an offshore account.
Anders told me that his winnings were "just for fun" and he didn't actually want to save that much so the only advice I gave this 20 year-old was to set aside 10% in a fixed interest rate account every time he won so we could talk later how to invest it.

I also asked him to decide how much he was willing to lose and win in percentage terms and to always stick to those figures. I only spoke to him the once but I would hear regularly from my brother about the apartments, Porsches, jewels and holidays Anders would buy. He took my brother on expensive trips to poker tournaments in Florida where he would spend days at the beach while Anders played.

It was some years later that I met Anders and by then he was totally broke. He had sold off everything and couldn't pay his rent. He was now asking my brother to give him a job.

He had never set any money aside, never mind investing in something that would accumulate more funds. He'd deemed that boring. He'd had ten years of frivolous spending and an unfinished university degree. Useless!

So if you decide to roll the dice and play in the big league, you must keep focused and retain the discipline that you had in the beginning. Remember, as I have already explained, the number one mistake people make when things are going well is to lose focus and start ignoring the needs of their clients and the market.

Going at speed can distract you from your financial status. I liken it to losing weight. A magazine article might tell you how to lose ten kilos in a week or fifteen kilos in a month, but do you think it is that easy?

After a week of barely eating and manic physical exercise you'll almost certainly shed the weight, only to gain it - plus a bit extra - at the same rate as soon as you start eating.

That's because you haven't done anything about changing the reasons behind why you put on weight in the first place.

You will only be able to make changes to your life - and stick to them - once you have set out a plan of what you intend to do and you really feel passionately about doing it.

Chapter 11

THE INVOLUNTARY ENTREPRENEUR

"Keep away from people who try to belittle your ambitions. Small people always do that, but the really great make you feel that you, too, can become great. When you are seeking to bring big plans to fruition, it is important with whom you regularly associate. Hang out with friends who are like-minded and who are also designing purpose-filled lives. Similarly be that kind of a friend for your friends."
- Mark Twain

I love to feel the wind in my face and my heart beating faster and faster. I can feel a frisson of fear as I teeter on the edge of losing control as my body leans as far to the ground as possible, getting an inch closer with every turn I make as I throw myself down the slope. Skiing is one of my favourite things in life and I never get bored of it. The world has so many mountains and slopes that I'll never get to experience them all in my lifetime, no matter how hard I try.

And you could say our journey through life is just like the skiing. There are those who will stick to the safe and easy slopes and there are those who will tackle the harder routes in order to test themselves and help each other grow in ability.

I often use skiing as a metaphor for running a business or making your dreams a reality. Standing at the top of any slope or mountain can be scary if you focus on the height, the vertical drop, the ice or just about anything but the beautiful view facing you.

Imagine how great you feel standing at the bottom having skied down a challenging slope. It all becomes so much easier.

I've come across many companies who have been skiing down the same slope for too long and are now at the bottom looking for an alternative way up. Imagine how great it would be if they had called me in to help them look to the horizon beyond before boredom struck and they lost all motivation to reach for the top by themselves. Boredom, as I've already said, is the ultimate culprit for scuppering your dreams.

It's also worth mentioning the global rise of what I call "involuntary entrepreneurs". These are the people who prove that anyone can create a good business, no matter the market or their past experience as long as their goals are firmly in focus and they are prepared to do what ever it takes to achieve them.

Involuntary entrepreneurs are not over-confident people who think that running a company is the easiest thing in the world. In fact they are the opposite. They know that it is not about turning their hobby into a well-functioning business just by registering a company, giving it a name and creating a website. They are normally quite reluctant to start a business.

Take Sophia for example, my dearest friend since we were sixteen. Sophia came to Sweden, with her parents and younger sister, as a six year-old refugee from Iran. The experience of going from everything to nothing and the chance of building something new had made her a real fighter.

We have always lived very differently but we both love to travel and have a zest for life. We've both been around the globe; Sophia for her humanitarian interests and me for financial opportunities. She always used to joke that she could live for a year upon what I spent in a month.

She has always been able to do anything she puts her mind to and I've always admired her tenacity in following her dream to be a journalist and writer.

A few years ago I met up with her after she had returned from the Middle East gathering stories depicting the lives of the region's women. Many publications wanted to buy the stories, but nobody actually wanted to employ her as a staff writer.

Previously the whole idea of being in business for herself had been an anathema but now she knew she had to change her attitude.

Change is good as long as you can manage it and changing yourself is one of the most manageable things you can do today. Sophia is far from being the only one who has had to learn how to think entrepreneurially.

Journalism is all about being first with the biggest news or breaking stories at the right times and editors are only going to pay the journalist who gets the story first rather than keeping a host of writers who don't on a retainer.

So there was Sophia, at the bottom of the ski slope with the right equipment, but not knowing really how anything worked or which slope to tackle first. I told her she could choose to stay safe on the easiest and flattest 'slopes' or leave her comfort zone and take a tougher route.

I reminded Sophia of a magazine for which she had written articles and asked her to think about its specific readership. As a freelance journalist, you need to make your articles interesting to a publication's readers so that they will want to buy it. One of the questions involuntary entrepreneurs find hardest to answer is why anyone should buy their products or services.

I knew however that Sophia really didn't need my help. Just as when she was sixteen and I'd taken her on her first ever ski trip, all I needed to do was give her a push and she'd get to the bottom on her own. She may not have done it in the finest style, but she did it on her own. I just needed to explain my thoughts when I created my own company and she would take what she needed from that to be a success on her own terms.

She had already written down her goals, she knew why she had to go out and grasp it and she had taken action by securing investors and planning her next assignment. She just hadn't seen the similarities of putting this together and running a company - but she did now.

Daniel one of my Danish clients dreamed about opening up a bistro in Antibes, in the south of France. A beautiful little town so who could blame him? I tried to tell him that even though he had the funds, running a bistro was not as easy and relaxing as it could seem from a guest's point of view. However he didn't heed my warning and went on to buy the bistro - only to find that he was pouring money in to a bottomless pit.

The bistro might have appeared to have an enormous potential but, like any other place in a popular tourist destination, there was enormous competition as well and in the end it required as much attention as all the rest of Daniel's projects.

Just as you have to demonstrate humility when working with people from other cultures, you have to respect other people's professions. If a restaurant looks as if it's a simple operation to run, it's probably because an awful lot of hard work has gone into making everything look so effortless.

"Nobody can make you feel inferior without your consent."
- Eleanor Roosevelt

For an involuntary entrepreneur, success is about being able to work with something you really feel passionate about. Success means different things to different people. There was a time when success was only measured by financial wealth, however times have changed and it is now closely tied to having the freedom to do what you enjoy most. Nelson Mandela once said: *"The greatest glory in living lies not in never falling, but in rising every time we fall."* Running a business is a great way of putting these words into practice.

Thanks to my dyslexia I had to find other strengths rather than worrying about fitting in with the system of getting good grades. I knew that I could succeed but I would always have a disadvantage when it came to writing - a big part of getting good grades. Dyslexics, or those with any other disability can choose to look at a problem and how they can be limited by it or focus on their strengths to overcome it. I chose the second option, just as many greater entrepreneurs and businesspeople have before me.

That afternoon on the terrace at the Ritz-Carlton in Singapore, I had felt as I did because I'd realised that I had to make a choice between doing what I loved most, which was growing as a person, or working for money. Paul had seen through me. He had seen that I was good at what I did but was not truly passionate about it. In the beginning, yes, because each challenge made me grow, but I had stopped achieving any personal growth. Only my bank account was growing. When I walked away from that meeting with Paul I knew I was saying goodbye to a very well paid job and hello to a life filled with freedom and passion. Since that day I have spent my time working only on projects I think I feel passionate about, helping others to realise their dreams. Helping others has given me the greatest satisfaction.

Success as an entrepreneur or businessperson is about ideas and excellence which cannot be measured in awards, or other people's approval. Surround yourself with people that will lift you higher and encourage you to reach your own goals no matter what they may be. The kind of people who will be there for you no matter how crazy your ideas may be.

When you are facing an important career choice and those important decisions that follow, focus on your own goals and don't be distracted by those of others. Do not let your old definition of success influence your choices for personal happiness, whether that is as an entrepreneur or an employee.

"Around here we don't look backwards for very long, we keep moving forward opening up new doors and doing new things because we're curious...and curiosity keeps leading us down new paths." - Walt Disney

Most new businesses do not even survive to the end of their first year and I have yet to meet a business owner or entrepreneur whose ideas were warmly received the first time round.

If you really have a burning desire to do something, put your goals down on paper and then start making them real.
Creating your business is no harder than learning how to ride a bike and, like riding a bike, you need to keep your head up to see what's on the road ahead and keep going whenever there's a hill to be negotiated. It won't always be easy but you're the one who gets to decide the length and fun of the ride.

SUMMARY

This is my story. I have combined my personal experiences and well-known examples from the world of international business to address the perceived problems when making a major shift in your life, whether in business or personal.

Each chapter identifies the necessary key tools and asks you to answer a number of questions.

Chapter 1 The road of life often starts with a question
The big question is "WHY" - if you can't answer this,
there's not much point continuing!

Chapter 2 Goals
Stop talking about what you want to do, start the process by identifying your goals and writing them down.

Chapter 3 Enjoying the moment
Don't let employment fool you into a sense of false security and lure you into boredom, ignite your passion and let it loose.

Chapter 4 Fear of rejection
Don't fear rejection, take charge of your own life story.

Chapter 5 Lift yourself higher!
Get to know yourself, your strengths and weaknesses and surround yourself with those who can inspire you.

Chapter 6 Creating relationships
Finding common ground, it takes two to tango!

Chapter 7 Keep your eyes on the horizon
Don't let previous success lull you into complacency, things change you know!

Chapter 8 Stepping out of your comfort zone

Sometimes leaving what you are used to can be hard for you and incomprehensible to others. Taking that step need not be so momentous if you are well prepared.

Chapter 9 Life, the great roller coaster!

Take the long view and don't lose site of your visions. If you get bogged down with daily tasks you won't realise what you have actually achieved during the year.

Chapter 10 Roll the dice

Calculated risks are really not that dramatic but combining passion with focus and planning could reduce drama later on.

Chapter 11 The involuntary entrepreneur

Many employed people already work as entrepreneurs, they just don't know it. Making that all important step is more psychological than anything else.

Through this book I have tried to introduce you to the immense joy and opportunities that await when you achieve success in business - or in life.

Don't forget, being indecisive will only see you going nowhere.

It's your life - choose how you live it!

APPENDIX

1. Goals - chapter 2

2. SWOT - chapter 5

3. Balance of Life - chapter 5

4. Circle of Life - chapter 5

5. Vision board - chapter 9

Goals - chapter 2

1. Business

2. Finance

3. Family

4. Health

5. Travel

SWOT - chapter 5

Swot _{strengths}	sWot _{weaknesses}
swOt _{opportunities}	swoT _{threats}

Balance of Life Chart - chapter 5

BALANCE OF LIFE CHART

TIME	HEALTH
1 - 2 - 3 - 4 - 5 - 6 - 7 - 8 - 9 - 10	1 - 2 - 3 - 4 - 5 - 6 - 7 - 8 - 9 - 10
PROFESSIONAL LIFE	RELATIONSHIPS
1 - 2 - 3 - 4 - 5 - 6 - 7 - 8 - 9 - 10	1 - 2 - 3 - 4 - 5 - 6 - 7 - 8 - 9 - 10
FINANCE	BALANCE OF LIFE (Add all the numbers entered for each category and divide by 5)
1 - 2 - 3 - 4 - 5 - 6 - 7 - 8 - 9 - 10	1 - 2 - 3 - 4 - 5 - 6 - 7 - 8 - 9 - 10

Circle of Life Chart - chapter 5

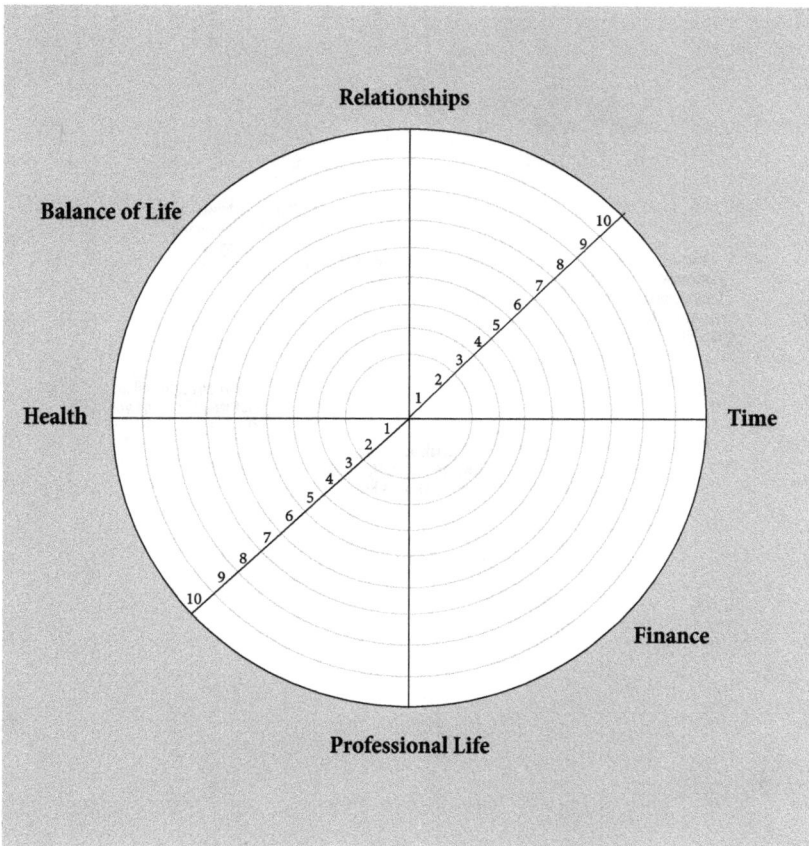

Relationships

Balance of Life

10
9
8
7
6
5
4
3
2
1

Health

1
2
3
4
5
6
7
8
9
10

Time

Finance

Professional Life

Vision Board - chapter 9

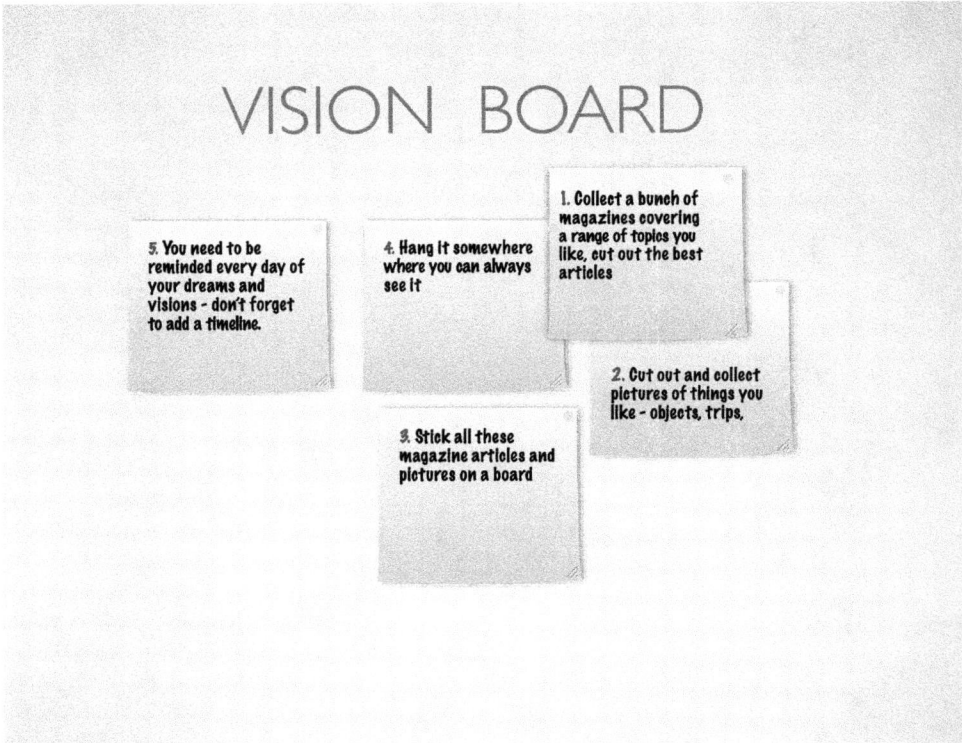

VISION BOARD

5. You need to be reminded every day of your dreams and visions - don't forget to add a timeline.

4. Hang it somewhere where you can always see it

1. Collect a bunch of magazines covering a range of topics you like, cut out the best articles

2. Cut out and collect pictures of things you like - objects, trips,

3. Stick all these magazine articles and pictures on a board

Notes

www.ingramcontent.com/pod-product-compliance
Lightning Source LLC
Chambersburg PA
CBHW071816020426
42331CB00007B/1504